Practical Handbooks in Archaeology
No 1

RECORDING WORKED STONES:
a practical guide

This manual has been compiled jointly by members of the Lapidary Working Party, established by the Churches Committee of the Council for British Archaeology. The principal contributors were Tom Blagg, Philip Lankester, Dr Richard K Morris (University of Warwick), Derek Phillips, Sarah Pollard, David Stocker and Jeffrey West. The drawings in section 5 were kindly provided by Bill Tidy. Dick Spicer assisted with Appendix IV. Editorial revision was undertaken by Richard Morris (University of Leeds) and David Stocker.

1987
Council for British Archaeology

Published 1987 by the Council for British Archaeology
112 Kennington Road, London SE11 6RE

British Library Cataloguing in Publication Data

Recording worked stones: a practical guide.
  (Practical handbooks in archaeology; no. 1)
  1. Building stones 2. Architecture
  3. Excavations (Archaeology)
  I. Council for British Archaeology.
  Lapidary Working Party   II. Series
  721'.0441   NA4130

  ISBN 0-906780-71-3

Typeset by Ann Buchan (Typesetters)
Printed by Henry Ling Ltd, Dorset Press, Dorchester

Contents

Illustrations and Tables

1 Introduction

1.0 Architectural fragments have always posed problems for the field archaeologist. On the site they are often too large and heavy for the finds table. They are difficult to mark effectively, and transporting them from site to store is usually difficult and sometimes hazardous. Once inside, they are often too large to be boxed, too heavy to be moved up or down stairs and often take up much valuable space when, finally, they are found a home. On some sites there will be a few choice pieces which find their way rapidly through the drawing office and into a place of honour in the site director's office, but the remainder, the great majority, await an uncertain academic future. In several field units, and in other institutions, a crisis is approaching, because all the available storage space has been used, and because there is no agreed procedure for dealing with the backlog. This manual does not offer solutions to all these difficulties, but it does suggest guidelines which, if followed, should make architectural fragments easier and quicker to process.

2 How to use this manual

2.0 First and foremost, the manual is designed to help those who excavate, investigate buildings, and have responsibility for the care, recording, publication, and long-term storage of finds. When the manual is being used in this functional way, the flow-chart (ch 3) will indicate the sequence of decisions and actions that will be appropriate to a given piece of stone.

2.1 It is also expected that the manual will have some value as an introduction to the study of worked stones. A small amount of theory and historical discussion is contained within, but it should be understood that the authors have not considered this to be the primary purpose of the document. Accordingly, the discussion of topics such as petrology and tooling has deliberately been kept to a minimum. If the academic aspects of lapidary studies are of interest to you, then the select bibliography at the end may be your best starting place.

2.2 Whatever your concern, please note that the key to the manual lies in Appendix I, where worked stones have been divided into categories. It is suggested that the needs in recording, publication, and storage of a particular stone should be determined by the category to which it is assigned. Until the categories have been memorized, it will be necessary to cross-refer between Appendix I and the main text.

2.3 When using the manual, please bear in mind that items which would be classified by archaeologists as 'small finds' are excluded. For those who are not familiar with archaeological jargon, a 'small find' is an artefact, other than a potsherd, which is of special interest or calls for separate treatment. Hence, a bronze pin, a coin, or a bone die would be regarded as a small find. Lapidary items which would also be so defined include spindle whorls, hones, ammunition for a *ballista*. Quernstones and mortaria are also regarded as meriting separate treatment, and so have been excluded from the manual. However, ecclesiastical fittings such as fonts, and fragments from monuments can be accepted under the general heading of 'architectural fragments'.

2.4 The bibliography is divided into seven numbered sections. Bibliographical references in the text are given with the section number in parentheses.

4 Categories of stone from an archaeological investigation

4.0 All recovered stone is of interest, and on many urban sites there will be a lot of it. The most basic division can be made at first inspection, into *cut* and *uncut* stone.

4.1 Uncut stone may be of petrological and/or geological interest. If a petrological study is thought to be worthwhile, a suitable specialist should be called in at an early stage and the stone collected as appropriate. There is no point in hoarding uncut stone unless a petrological study is envisaged.

4.2 Cut stone should be divided into several categories. Non-architectural items (ie 'small finds' – see 2.3, above) should be segregated at once. Many problems may arise later on if all stone finds are entered in the same register.

4.3 The cut stone now remaining may be regarded as architectural, and should belong within categories 1–5 in Appendix I.

5 Handling stones and personal safety

5.0 It is impossible to give comprehensive advice on matters of handling and safety here. All users of this manual are therefore urged to consult relevant publications and advisory leaflets on health, safety, lifting and carrying *before* embarking upon excavations or programmes of recording. A small selection of such publications will be found in the bibliography.

5.1 Many stones have rough or jagged surfaces. When stones are handled there is thus a high risk of scratches, scrapes or more serious injuries, which may occur both on site *and* indoors, for instance during transfers of stones to, from or within the temporary store, or even in the drawing office.

Fig   1   Do not leave stones lying where they can cause accidents (Bill Tidy)

Directors should ensure that those who handle stones wear appropriate clothing (eg industrial gloves and reinforced footwear). They should also see that everyone involved has checked on the need for an anti-tetanus injection.

Basic first aid provision should be made for deep cuts, large open wounds, breaks and strains. For advice on what the first aid kit should contain, consult (6) CBA 1972, esp 12–13.

Fig 2 *Take precautions against scrapes and abrasions. Is your immunization against tetanus up to date? (Bill Tidy)*

Fig 3 *Check that the first-aid kit is properly stocked (Bill Tidy)*

5.2 Never lift anything if the action is likely to lead to injury. Avoid lifting from an awkward posture. Do not strain. Ensure that both hands have a good grip. Do not try to lift using fingertips alone (eg using a rebate or moulding of slight projection), for if the stone slips a serious accident may result. When lifting a stone, check beforehand that the person(s) involved can manage the job comfortably. If two or more people are needed, always make sure that each of them knows exactly what s/he is to do, and that the lift is properly coordinated. When lifting, the usual technique is to keep the body close to the stone and lift with the legs, *not* the back. Once the stone is raised, the knees should take the weight, the arms should be tucked well in, and the body kept straight. Throughout, the golden rule is 'know your limitations'.

Fig 4   Know your limitations (Bill Tidy)

5.3 Stones should never be thrown. Such action may cause injury to a person – and it may damage the stone.

5.4 If a hoist or pulley is used to lift a stone from an excavation, workers guiding the ascent must wear safety helmets. They should stand as far back as possible while the hoist/pulley is in use. Prevent the stone from swinging back and forth, which may cause injury, or damage the side of the excavation. Ensure that the hoist operator is thoroughly proficient with the equipment before any attempt is made to lift a stone in this way.

Fig 5 Observe proper precautions when machinery is used (Bill Tidy)

6 Cleaning, marking, and temporary storage

Cleaning

6.0 Before a worked stone can be recorded accurately, some cleaning may be necessary. This should be undertaken only with guidance from a qualified conservator. Such advice is called for because a range of deposits (eg limewash, pigment, mortar) may be preserved. Sometimes the presence of mortar on display faces will be the only evidence that a piece has been reused. Surface deposits may easily be removed by indiscriminate cleaning. If the stone is weathered, its surface may be fragile, and careless cleaning can cause loss of surface and moulded detail.

6.1 Excavated stones bearing large areas of limewash, pigment and/or mortar should be kept in conditions which as far as possible are akin to those from which they have just been removed and referred to a conservator as soon as possible. For advice on packing, see (5) Leigh (1978 or forthcoming). In most cases this will mean an environment which is slightly damp, cool, and dark. Fine silt covering a painted surface can be almost impossible to remove if it is allowed to dry out and harden. Some pigments will fade if they are not protected from daylight. The growth of micro-organisms on the surface will be inhibited if the object is kept as cool as possible.

6.2 Fragments where pigment is expected but not immediately obvious should also be referred to a conservator for cleaning. Pigment which survives under salt crystals and concretions may not be discovered unless cleaning is carefully controlled and takes place under a microscope.

6.3 If some cleaning on site is absolutely necessary, and the stone bears no obvious surface deposit, cleaning should be limited to the removal of loose dirt. If the surface is allowed to dry, such material can be dusted away with a soft brush or removed with the fingers or a softwood dowel.

6.4 If, following consultation with the conservator, the stone is shown to be sound and unpainted, and further cleaning is still required, distilled water can be used and applied with cotton wool swabs or a soft bristle stencil brush.

6.5 Never use metal or wire brushes – they damage the surface and there is a risk of corrosion staining the stone. On no account should a piece be immersed in water; a stone which looks sound may nevertheless be damaged if it is submerged. This applies especially to weathered sedimentary rocks, eg some New Sandstones, many limestones, chalk, and alabaster, which is soluble in water.

Marking

6.6 Once a stone has been removed from its archaeological context, it is vital that it should be adequately marked. It is recommended that stones should be marked three times, in the hope that at least one mark will survive even in poor storage conditions. Regular checks should be made and faded marks replaced.

6.7 Remember that an effective marking method may not be aesthetically acceptable. Moreover, indiscriminate application of paint or labels could mask or cause damage to surface detail or pigment.

6.8 Hitherto no satisfactory universal method of marking has been found. The viability of any method will vary according to the type of stone (see Table 1), its condition, and the circumstances under which it is stored. In many cases a standard artists' acrylic paint will be suitable. Application by brush is normally best, although a pen may be usable on hard, smooth surfaces. Where possible, marks should be applied to broken surfaces. If no such surface is available, use a surface that would originally have been concealed.

6.9 The marking of pieces which are destined for reburial is a particular problem. No paint or label will last indefinitely. The only permanent way to mark these stones may be to engrave them.

6.10 For quick, easy identification during storage a plastic label may be tied on, using plastic cord. However, such labels should never be the only means of identification, as they are easily lost. Bagging and boxing may be feasible for some stones; boxes are easy to label and store, and the stones are protected from damage, dust and dirt. If plastic bags are used, they must have holes to permit circulation of air. Stones must be dry before bagging to minimize the risk of mould growth; they should be bagged individually in order to avoid abrasion. Freezer bags are best. For larger stones reinforced open-weave sacks such as those used by farmers and coal merchants are recommended. Plastic crates, boxes or trays of the kinds used in supermarkets are tough and easy to label.

Storage

6.11 Stones are not indestructible. If they are left in unsuitable conditions they will deteriorate. Stones left outside may be vulnerable to frost damage, wind erosion, chemical attack, as well as ill effects caused by algae, lichen, fungi and micro-organisms. Indoors physical and chemical deterioration can occur if stones are not protected from extremes of relative humidity, temperature, and atmospheric pollution. To illustrate: cycles of high and low relative humidity cause corresponding cycles of dissolution and precipitation of soluble salts, with accompanying volume changes which disrupt the stone structure. Dust and dirt may contribute to moisture accumulation. In moist layers dissolved dirt can react as an acid or an alkali. Dust particles also cause discolouration of the surfaces.

6.12 The post-excavation storage of worked stone can be divided into three phases: on site; temporary storage during recording; long-term storage or disposal.

On site

6.12.1 Stones should be kept under cover, preferably indoors, but at least under tarpaulins or plastic sheet to protect them from the weather, bird droppings, abrasion, etc. The covering should be loose enough to permit the circulation of air in order to minimize condensation. Stones need to be isolated from damp. Hence, they should not be placed directly on the ground but upon planks or palettes. The latter will also make the movement of large stones with a fork-lift truck easier, and safer both for the stone

Table 1 The effects and effectiveness of marking methods on stones of different kinds: a sample list

Stone type	Operator	direct	Ink over PVA base	Ink over paint	Direct paint	Result	Disadvantage
Carboniferous	1 YMAO			★[1]		Good	Disfiguring
	2 Various	★				Moderate –poor	Fading, abrasion
Millstone grit, sandstone	3 Various	★				Poor	Fading, abrasion
	4 Various		★			Moderate –poor	PVA prone to peel
	5 Various			★		Moderate –good	Disfiguring
	6 YMAO			★[1]		Good	
Lower carboniferous sandstone ('York' stone): Pennines	7 Various	★				Moderate –poor	Fading, abrasion
	8		★			Moderate –poor	PVA adheres only with difficulty
Carboniferous sandstone: Gloucs (Pennant)	9 BAT	★				Moderate	PVA prone to peel
Permian Magnesian limestone	10 Various	★				Moderate –good	Fades
	11 Various		★			Moderate –good	
	12 YMAO			★[1]		Good	Disfiguring
	13 YMus			★		Good	Disfiguring
Jurassic Marlestone (Lias) (Northants, Lincs)	14 Various	★				Moderate –poor	
	15 Various		★			Moderate –poor	PVA prone to peel
Blue Lias	16 TLA	★				Good	

Stone type	Operator	direct	Ink over PVA base	Ink over paint	Direct paint	Result	Disadvantage
Jurassic Great & inferior oolite ser ('Bath stone')	17 BAT		★			Moderate	PVA prone to peel
	18 DOE	★				Moderate	
Great & inferior oolite ser	19 Various	★				Moderate –good	
(Clipsham, Ancaster, Lincoln)	20 YMAO				★[1]	Good	
	21 YMAO		★			Moderate –good	PVA prone to peel
Great & inferior oolite ser (Barnack)	22 Various	★				Poor	Surface too irregular
	23 Various		★			Moderate –poor	If sound base is applied, some success
Cretaceous Green sandstone (Wiltshire outcrops)	24 DoE	★				Moderate –good	Fades
'Carstone' (Lincs & Norfolk outcrops)	25 TLA	★				Poor	
	26 TLA		★			Poor	
Chalk ('Lincolnshire clunch')	27 TLA	★				Poor	
	28 TLA		★			Poor	
'Marbles' 'Purbeck'–Jurassic 'Alwalton'–Jurassic	29 Various	★				Moderate –good	
'Frosterly'–Carbonif	30 Various		★			Moderate –good	
	31 YMus				★	Good	Disfiguring

[1] White enamel on red primer background

BAT — Bath Archaeological Trust
Doe — Department of the Environment (now English Heritage)
TLA — Trust for Lincolnshire Archaeology
YMAO — York Minster Archaeology Office
YMus — Yorkshire Museum

and for the person who transports it. Stones should not be piled on top of each other; surfaces will be damaged and individual stones will be difficult to locate and retrieve.

Temporary storage

6.12.2 Facilities for the housing of archaeological material vary from place to place. The following recommendations are therefore divided into two groups: *minimum requirements*, and conditions which are regarded as *ideal*.

Minimum requirements
Stones should be isolated from sources of damp, protected from the elements, and from extremes of relative humidity and temperature. They should be placed on sheet plastic foam, to reduce risk of damage from abrasion. They should never be piled on top of each other (see 6.12.1).

Shelving must be of wood rather than metal, and of suitable strength. If neither shelves nor palettes are available, fragments should at least be placed on a damp-proof membrane such as sheet plastic. As far as possible free circulation of air around the stones should be maintained. It is also advisable to cover fragments to protect them from dust, light, bird droppings, etc.

Ideal conditions
The building or room used as a temporary stone store should at least comply with the minimum standards set out by the Archaeology Section (5) UKIC (1983) for a basic store suitable for building materials. That is, it should (1) be structurally sound; (2) allow easy access, both to the building and to the stones inside; (3) not be liable to damp, leaks, flooding, gross pollutants (eg boiler fumes), excessive vibration, temperature changes, or infestations; (4) have a relative humidity between 40% and 70%, with only gradual fluctuations; (5) have a temperature which should not fall below 4°C (39°F) or exceed 30°C (86°F); (6) exclude direct sunlight upon the materials stored. The conditions inside the store should be monitored by a conservator.

Long-term storage

This involves considerations apart from those to do with conservation. Accordingly, long-term storage is dealt with separately, in chapter 9.

7 The recording of cut stone

7.0 An archive record must be produced for each item of cut stone. What follows is a description of the type of archive record now in use at a number of places. It is presented as a series of notes on a method that has proved to be useful in the field, and that, most importantly, has enabled the rapid dispatch of large collections of material.

7.1 The aim of this procedure is the production of a *usable archive* of records, *not* a final publication. It is regrettable that in the past detailed records have often been made only of those pieces for which publication was intended. Of course, items from the archive can be selected for publication. The archive drawing scheme is designed to be operated by non-specialist draftsmen, but these drawings provide a workable basis for publication drawings which may be produced by specialists.

7.2 The method is a response to the assumption that a considerable percentage of the material recorded will not be readily accessible in the future (see ch 9). The archive has thus been designed to record the maximum amount of usable information with the minimum of effort.

7.3 Appendix II illustrates a detailed scheme that has been in use since 1978, and that has evolved to take account of difficulties encountered in the field. What follows now is a general description of requirements for an adequate archive record. Appendix II shows how these requirements can be translated into a practical working scheme. Other translations are possible.

7.4 It is considered that an adequate archive record has four components: written, drawings, photograph(s), tooling.

Written record

7.5.1 Each cut fragment is best provided with a card, or computer entry, carrying a written record of the piece in question. The amount of information will obviously vary according to the relative significance of the item, but as a minimum each should carry (1) the record number of the stone and its accompanying context reference, etc; (2) the type of stone in use, some indication of the minimum and maximum dimensions; (3) a description of architectural and other features (including mention of cramp holes etc, and a note on tool marks, if these are present).

The card will also carry cross references to the files of drawings, photographs, and tooling records (7.5.2–4, below). Part of the card ought to be available for an architectural analysis. The completed card forms the basic record for each piece of stone. Other types of record can be used in conjunction with it to complete an archive record.

Archive drawings

7.5.2 There is no standard method for archive or publication drawings of architectural fragments. Techniques range from elementary diagrams to lovingly crafted drawings that attempt to show every toolmark and abrasion. We must ask which type of drawing records most information about an architectural fragment, and proceed from there.

Architectural fragments are seldom recovered in mint condition. They are almost always scraped, and part of the detail is often missing. It is therefore necessary to aim at a drawing style that gives an appropriate impression of the condition of the stone, but avoids obscuring the remains of critical original boundaries between planes by giving them the same visual 'weight' as accidental damage.

In practice it is convenient to divide fashioned stones into two groups for the purposes of producing record drawings: (a) stonework carrying sculpture (ie categories 1 and 2.3 in Appendix I); (b) stonework carrying mouldings and other non-sculptural features (ie categories 2–4 in Appendix I)

Architectural sculpture

Stones in this group are usually important enough to merit considerable drafting time. The drawing styles employed for such pieces at present are mostly an adequate response to the challenges posed, and as time is not usually a significant consideration (because of the importance of the items), this group need not detain us. As with other types of stone, however, a separate *tooling record* (7.5.4, below) for pieces of architectural sculpture is advisable.

Stonework carrying non-sculptural decoration or other features

This group will usually contain the majority of pieces. Consequently the length of time taken in the production of record drawings is an important consideration.

Drawing layout

The architectural information carried by each stone will almost always be best depicted by a number of plans, elevations, and sections. In general these are best drawn without perspective, two views being preferable to one view showing two faces together. The views should be chosen in order to show the critical aspects of each stone, and not according to any predetermined scheme. For some simple pieces a single view and a section will suffice; for others a larger number of drawings will be needed.

Sections require thoughtful treatment, which may depart from current methods. Sections of architectural fragments are commonly drawn according to the 'hypothetical slice' principle. However, while a well chosen 'hypothetical slice' may be appropriate for other categories of find, it is often inappropriate for a stone. Therefore a *composite section* is usually best. This means a section built up from small 'cuts' through a number of different parts of the stone. The section may not exist in any given plane of the surviving stone; it will instead show what a single slice would have looked like if the stone had been preserved intact. However, it should be noted that the composite section will be a reconstruction founded upon evidence that *does* survive, albeit in different parts of the stone.

The composite slice conflicts with a basic principle of archaeological draftsmanship, namely that the drawing should depict what is there today. Accordingly, a conventional single-slice section may also be included, but will probably be of less value to the architectural historian than its composite counterpart. Composite sections should be clearly labelled as such, to avoid any risk of confusion with ordinary sections.

Drawing scale
Record drawings of architectural fragments are best drawn at 1:1. This is quicker, and means that small but important details can be included. It also makes the reconstruction of architectural features and cross-referencing with other pieces much easier. If such record drawings have to be reduced for publication, pen widths should be selected accordingly.

Drawing technique
Different draftsmen will develop their own styles for architectural masonry. No single method should be thought of as being 'correct', but general comments may be helpful.

Shading When architectural fragments have been regarded as small finds, shading has been used to attempt a depiction of their surface condition. Shading, however, cannot represent tooling adequately (see 7.5.4, below) and causes confusion to the eye when significant architectural information is sought on a surface of accidental breaks and abrasions. Shading to depict surface texture is thus generally inadvisable. It is also unnecessary for record purposes, and time-consuming to execute.

Shading to indicate the curvature of a moulded face can be effective, although a result of the temptation to emphasize major concavities can be that minor boundaries get lost. The line of the arris (boundary) in such cases is usually more important than the visual appearance of the concavities, the exact proportions of which will be shown to much better advantage on a section.

To summarize, tactful shading to express the relative depths of surface features may be desirable, but is not as important as the positions, directions and sections of arrises and other mouldings, and should not be allowed to interfere with them visually. The specimen record drawings in Appendix I contain no shading at all. If necessary, shading can be added to publication drawings at a later stage.

Boundary lines Boundaries between different planes are not best depicted by shading alone. Since these arrises are often critical for purposes of dating, or in ascertaining the position of a piece within a larger architectural feature, their position and orientation must be shown exactly and clearly. What is needed, therefore, is a method of drawing which differentiates between arrises and other boundaries.

Most pieces will present one or more of the following: cut surfaces meeting at arrises, incised lines (such as laying-out lines or tooling marks), breaks and damaged areas. It is also probable that parts of the detail will need to be reconstructed. If reconstruction is not attempted, then the points at which missing parts of the original feature connected with what survives will need to be indicated.

An economical system will employ different types of line (broken, ruled, dotted, etc) for different kinds of boundary. Such a system gives accurate depictions of mouldings, and presents information in a format that is easily comprehended by those who wish to make use of it. A further advantage lies in the speed with which an archive of ready-to-use drawings can be produced by non-specialist draftsmen.

Photographic records

7.5.3 A photograph will seldom be sufficient as the only visual record of a stone. Drawings (see 7.5.2, above) provide a much more accurate and versatile record. Of course, photographs form a useful and necessary component of the archive, but they are best thought of as *adjuncts* to the drawings, not as substitutes.

Good photographs will make an excellent index to a collection. They can also be used in place of drawings at a superficial level of consultation. Some pieces, especially stones of high sculptural quality, will need an extensive photographic record to complement the drawings; photographs can capture aspects of such items that are hard to catch in a drawing.

A photograph may be acceptable as a substitute for a drawing for some stones in categories 3, 4, and 5 (Appendix I). But even in these cases a drawing will be more useful than a photograph if comparisons are to be made between the records of different stones. Advice on taking photographs of stones is given in Appendix III.

Tooling records

7.5.4 Studies of medieval tooling are in their infancy. There is no large body of research to which reference can be made. The range of tools in use in the Roman and medieval periods is known, and the marks which many of these implements made on stone can now be identified. However, when the tool used on a stone is recognized, can such information be of any further use, for example, for dating? The answer is that it probably can, but the degree of accuracy is not yet known.

There is no doubt that styles of tooling changed through time, but the patterns of these changes are not yet known. Certainly the changes are not uniform across the country. They are affected, as might be expected, by the geology in the area of production, and by differing regional traditions. In each stone area a large number of tooling samples from dated structures are needed before anything more than generalizations can be offered about the date of a particular stone simply from the evidence of its tooling. At present tooling is at its most useful where it occurs on pieces of known provenance and/or date.

Tooling can often be recorded satisfactorily by rubbings, provided that a suitable wax and paper are found; different weights of paper and textures of wax are suited to different types of stone and toolmark. A postcard size is usually sufficient. The rubbing may preserve information about the type of blade used and the size of tool. If it can be ascertained, the relationship of the toolmarks to the bed of the stone ought to be noted.

For pieces where the only interest lies in their tooling, a photograph and/or rubbing will usually suffice as the visual record. Detail will be enhanced by the use of a cutting light (see Appendix III). Photographic recording will also be necessary for the coarser stones, some of which are too granular to accept a rubbing, and where the tool marks may be large. Pieces carrying fine or unusual specimens of tooling may deserve detail photographs.

Once the tooling and written records have been prepared, there is no reason why a stone which is otherwise without interest should not be discarded (see ch 9).

8 Publication

8.0 Completed record drawings will provide a basis for publication drawings. They will need to be carefully shaded and reduced. Such drawings have been satisfactorily employed in many recent publications, combined with a written catalogue, general comments on the significance of the pieces to the archaeology of the site, and on their own architectural importance.

8.1 In some quarters, however, there is a persistent tendency to look upon architectural fragments as finds pure and simple, and to relegate them to appendices or finds volumes in company with hones, querns, mortars, and other stone artefacts. This approach fails to recognize that architectural fragments, in addition to their intrinsic interest, are usually of greater archaeological significance than small finds. Unlike hones or querns, architectural fragments on most sites were often used in the construction of the building(s) under excavation. They are as much a part of the stratification as the deposits with which they may be associated. The published account of architectural fragments is therefore best placed for consideration alongside the archaeology.

8.2 This approach is completely vindicated when architectural fragments are discussed in conjunction with the excavation report, because they often provide information for the excavator. Firstly, they can indicate the former appearance of the building which originally stood on the substructure, and they can sometimes date the building with considerable accuracy. Secondly, where fragments are reused in later buildings (an extremely common occurrence in towns) they can provide valuable terminal dates.

9 Long-term storage

The long-term storage of worked stone presents problems which have hardly been considered, let alone solved, and which are arguably beyond both the brief and the means of most field archaeology units and archaeological societies. The matter needs to be addressed by local authorities, cathedral fabric committees, HBMC, Cadw, SDD, and other bodies which have custody of and responsibility for the care of lapidary material. The issue was mentioned in the Longworth Report, but only briefly and with many aspects left unconsidered.

The points made here are confined to two broad possibilities: (1) storage above ground, perhaps in large disused buildings, such as aircraft hangars, which would be suitable for conversion; and (2), storage by reburial.

Storage above ground

9.1 A long-term store should at the very least meet the recommended standards for a temporary store listed above (section 6.12.2). Ideally the building would comply with the target standards described in the UKIC publication ((5) 1984).

Reburial

9.2 The British Museum working party ((5) 1982) Longworth) suggested that certain categories of worked stone could be reburied after records had been made. Although at first glance this may not seem an attractive option, it is certainly better than the fate to which many excavated fragments are currently condemned. Longworth proposed that the more architecturally significant pieces should be preserved above ground, with reburial for the rest as an acceptable option, given present shortages of funds and space. It should, however, be remembered that buried objects move towards an equilibrium with their environment; once in this state, the rate of deterioration is likely to be minimized. It cannot be guaranteed that this balance will be restored upon reburial – at least not before further deterioration has occurred, particularly if the stone is reburied on a different site.

Items should not be reburied without research into the suitability of the site, with regard to level of water table; drainage; pH of soil; ease of recovery; type of stone being reburied (eg whether it will be compatible with the soil type); security of site.

Geologically different stones will require different conditions. A further point to bear in mind is whether the digging of a large hole will cause archaeological damage. The last thing wanted will be another archaeological excavation!

In summary, the merits and drawbacks of reburial as a means of storing of stones have hardly been assessed. So far stones have been reburied on a few guardianship sites, but none have yet been recovered and the long-term effects are unknown. More research is needed before this method of disposal becomes common practice; reburial can only be entertained for stones which have been properly recorded, along lines explained above.

Appendix I Categories of worked stone

This is a brief survey of the main categories of worked stones from an architectural context encountered on Roman and medieval sites. It is followed by a concise guide to the minimum recording procedure for each category. The categories are intended primarily for guidance with recording, and need not be regarded as exclusive. One should always be on the lookout for possible relationships between stones in several categories, derived from a common architectural context. Some examples are illustrated here; for illustrations and descriptions of other types of stone from architectural contexts consult the CBA *Glossary* ((4) Cocke *et al* 1984).

1 Sculpture

Definition This category comprises (a) free-standing sculpture (eg statuary); (b) sculpture where the architectural context is unknown; (c) sculpture where the architectural context is known, but which has no mouldings or other features to connect it with category 2 (eg carved fragments from a Romanesque tympanum, or from a temple pediment).

2 Mouldings

Definition stones on which the primary or sole embellishment is the carving of abstract architectural forms of continuous section.

2.1 Roman

The chief distinction to be made is between elements that were originally placed horizontally and others used vertically. Among the former, capitals, bases, and the elements from an entablature are frequently identifiable, while among the latter are fragments from columns.

2.2 Medieval

These architectural remains are more numerous and more complex than those from the Roman period. Hence, a more extensive classification may be adopted, according to the architectural context (where this is discoverable). The following classifications are applicable both to architecture and to monuments/fittings, with scale as an important guide to context.

Apertures
Examples are arcades, doors, fireplaces, sedilia. Distinguish between mouldings used *vertically*, and *arched* or *horizontal* mouldings.

Examples of vertical mouldings include: piers, columns, responds, jambs, or uprights of fittings, tomb canopies; door jambs (look for the large rebate for door fittings (Fig 6a)); window mullions and jambs of window frames (look for glass slot or small rebate for glass (Fig 6b)). Some of the above features are free-standing (eg piers, mullions), while others are attached to walls (eg responds, door-frames). Well preserved stones should contain clues to their context.

1

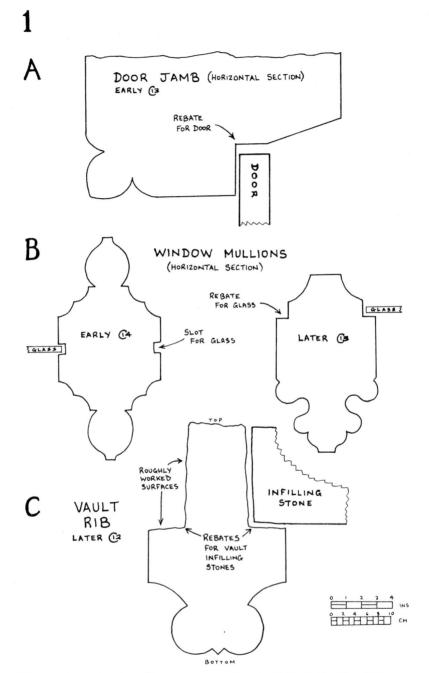

Fig 6 Recognizing mouldings: apertures and vaults (R K Morris, Warwick)

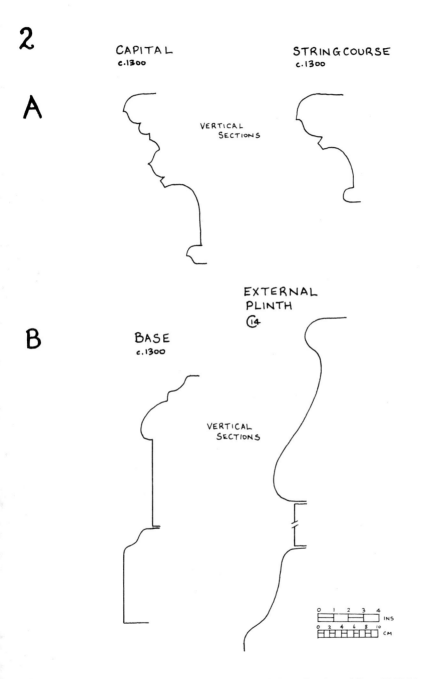

Fig 7 Recognizing mouldings: capitals, bases, and their related mouldings (R K Morris, Warwick)

Examples of arched or horizontal mouldings include: arcade arches, colonnade lintels, heads of fittings or tomb canopies; door heads (look for rebate, cf door jambs, above); window heads and arches of window frames (look for glass slots or small rebates).

Capitals and related mouldings
Capitals and corbels generally share similar moulding designs with stringcourses and hoodmoulds (Fig 7a). To distinguish between them, the former are *centralized* in plan (square, circular, polygonal), whereas the latter continue in the same plane and are thus generally flat.

Bases and related mouldings
Bases generally share similar moulding designs with foundation or plinth mouldings. The combinations of these mouldings are generally different to those employed for capitals, string courses, etc (Fig 7b). As with capitals, bases are centralized in plan, whereas foundation and plinth mouldings continue in the same plane for some distance and are thus generally flat.

Vaults
Tangible evidence will almost invariably come from rib vaults of the Gothic period. Earlier vaults of the groin or tunnel type, built mainly from rubble, will be difficult to identify from fragments. The main components from rib vaults are the ribs and cells. *Ribs* often have mouldings which are similar to other architectural features (especially mullions in the later medieval period), but they are sometimes distinguished by pairs of rebates behind the mouldings, to take the cell infilling. Ribs generally have rebates after the mid 13th century, and the rebates are normally deeper and more crudely finished than those for doors (Fig 6c). Look for curvature appropriate to the context of a vault, but remember that ridge ribs will generally be straight.

Note that some late Gothic and Tudor vaults, as well as miniature vaults, have the rib and cell units carved from the same block of stone. Look for the surface of the cell adjoining the rib at 90° at the point where the rebate would be cut in a conventional vault.

Worked stones for infilling the *cells* will be unmoulded, often trapezoidal, and might be classified under category 3 (below) unless their real context is recognized.

Miscellaneous
Examples include: pinnacles (often decorated with foliage crockets); parapets, sometimes pierced with open tracery decorations; coping stones, to cap parapets and other walltops.

Note that certain moulded stones will be so fragmentary that it may not be possible to assign them to any category. However, if such stones can be grouped according to moulding design, this may help to establish links with other pieces. For Gothic mouldings, a useful visual division can often be made between moulding formations based on roll mouldings (shafts/bowtells), often alternating with deep hollow mouldings, and those based on mouldings that adhere closely to the chamfer plane (eg chamfer, hollow chamfer, sunk chamfer, and wave mouldings). Consult the bibliography (3) for works that describe and illustrate moulding types.

2.3   Decoration

During the Roman and medieval periods, various types of carved decoration were used in conjunction with mouldings. These include conventionalized motifs such as Roman egg and dart, or medieval chevron and ballflower ornament. Also to be grouped here is representational sculpture (human, animal, foliate) where this is employed in a strictly architectonic context, such as a Roman frieze, or a medieval label-stop. Where such pieces can be linked with one of the classifications in 2.1 or 2.2 in this Appendix (above), they should be catalogued with them, and *not* in category 1 (sculpture).

3   Worked stones with two or more faces at other than 90°

Definition   stones which have no trace of sculpture or mouldings, and are not squared ashlars (see category 4), but have at least two worked faces (cf category 5). Stones in this class are often fragments from larger pieces which, if complete, might have incorporated sculpture or mouldings and thus have been classified under categories 1 or 2, above.

In recording, it is important to make a distinction between pieces that include tooling or other evidence of masoncraft, and pieces devoid of such features, often because of wear or deterioration.

4   Worked stones with two or more faces at 90° ($\pm$)

Definition   these stones will usually be either squared ashlars, or squared fragments from larger stones which, if complete, might have incorporated sculpture or mouldings and thus have been catalogued in categories 1 or 2, above.

In recording, it is important to make a distinction between pieces that bear tooling or other evidence of masoncraft, and pieces devoid of such features, often because of wear or deterioration.

5   Worked stones with only one tooled face

Definition   stones with only a single tooled face, and upon which no other architectural or stylistic features survive. Many excavated fragments fit only this description.

Note that in all the above categories, attention should be paid also to the recording of holes and other features pertaining to structure or construction, eg dowel holes in column drums or statuary, holes for attaching Lewis lifting gear to large stones, etc. See further the Bibliography.

Guide to record types
The types of record referred to in this table are explained in Appendix II. The drawing of architectural sculpture is mentioned in the main text, (ch 7).

Table 2   Record types recommended for different categories of worked stone

Stone Category	Record Card	Archit sculp	Mouldings (App II)		Photo(s)	Tooling
1 Sculpture	★	★			★	(★)
2 Mouldings	★	(★)	★		★	(★)
3 Two or more faces, other than 90°	★		★	OR	★	(★)
4 Two or more faces at 90°	★		★	OR	★	(★)
5 One worked or tooled face only	★				(★)	(★)

(★) = if appropriate

Appendix II A detailed scheme for recording

Below is a detailed scheme for the production of an archive record of large collections of architectural fragments. The system has been developed over a number of years, according to principles discussed in chapter 7. The intention throughout will be to give a schematic representation of the appearance of each piece, where possible reconstructing its original form, and paying particular attention to moulded detail and tooling.

RECORDING

For each stone there will be at least three of the following types of record: (1) written; (2) drawn; (3) other visual record (usually photo); (4) tooling sample(s).

1 Entry on record card (fig 8)

Every stone will have its own record card. Ideally the card will be of a type which will enable the computerization of the architectural fragments from the site, along with the other finds.

The card will record: (a) site; (b) find number; (c) contextual information; (d) present location; (e) material; (f) maximum dimensions; (g) abbreviated name; (h) description (including tooling); (i) earliest/latest probable dates; (j) indication of dating method used; (k) analytical discussion; (l) cross references. Other entries may be provided for.

2 Drawings (Fig 9)

2.1 Drawings in line

Types of drawing required will be dictated by the character of the stone in question. In all cases, however, there will be at least two of the following: plan, view from above, view from below, elevation, section of 'actual' type, section of 'composite' type (see 7.5.2b).

Where it is possible to reconstruct part or the whole of the feature from which a piece comes (eg to reconstruct an arch from one *voussoir*) this will be done separately, to a different scale, and will be cross-referenced to the routine archive record (Fig 10).

Scales Wherever possible drawings are to be actual size (1:1).

Method Unless otherwise stated, elevations and views will be drawn *without* regard for perspective (ie drawings deal with only one face at a time). This means that two drawings are preferred to one which shows a second face in perspective-affected condition. The standpoint of an elevation relative to its section/plan/view is shown by its relative position on the page (Fig 9). For archive purposes there will be no stippling to show the contours of a piece, as these will be shown by the appropriate section, plan, or view.

2	St. 49			1	D.T. 74 I
3	H.Q.			5	Jurassic limestone of local Lincolnshire character.
4	T.L.A. LINCOLN			6	

7 — MOULDED SHAFT CAPITAL — A pentangular Block incorporating a small moulded shaft capital at one end. The cap is of circular plan and has a double-chamfered astragal. A neck of "bell" type develops into a hollow-chamfered rim under a band of nailhead. The chamfered abacus is of square plan. The underside of the stem behind the cup is chamfered on both 8 [?] sides, the rear is mitred.

Setting-out lines on F.1+F.4; one No1 on F5 [partly missing]; compossible in F.4.
Tooling. —F1,2,3,4,6+7 — med Diag claws, sometimes X
—F5 —traces of fine claws + Drag [Not Recorded]
F.5 is slightly weathered.

9	1190 × 1230	10	Moulding Form — cap Square Abacus.

11 — This cup stood over a free-standing shaft and projected boldly from the wall in which it was set. It projected to the same extent as the pair of bases Nos 61 + 62 which also carried a shaft of the same dia. These bases are thus probably from the same orig. feature. All come from a blind arcade. The five archend sections Sts. Nos. 1,4,59,62,64 are probably also from this arcade [they were found in related contexts] and springer block St 59 fits cup 49 comfortably.
The arcade is of the same date as windows S-65 and Doorway L-55 and may have originated in the same building.

12 — See DT74 I/Sts. Nos 61 +63 : SRecord. 3

Fig 8   *The archive: specimen record card (Trust for Lincolnshire Archaeology)*

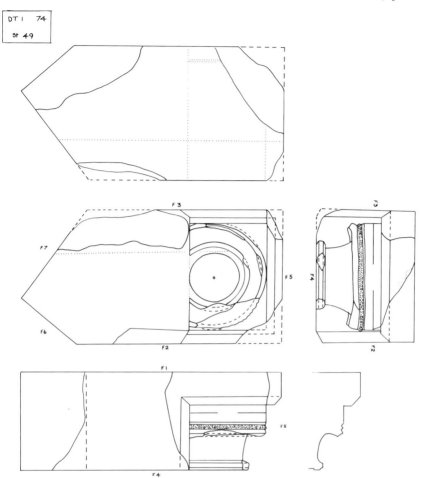

Fig 9 The archive: a set of record drawings (originals drawn at 1:1)

Lines used as conventions (Fig 9)

Erratic lines will represent *broken edges* and *unintentional* boundaries of cut surfaces. It is normally clear on which side of the erratic line the cut surface lies. Accidental (ie uncut) features in a broken area on the surface of a stone are not shown. Erratic lines will take a generalized form; while they preserve the overall appearance of a stone, they are not intended to be a detailed representation.

Non-erratic lines, either straight or curved, represent *intentional* boundaries and arrises, even those that are roughly cut (the quality will be described on the record card). Cut boundaries and arrises are usually detectable on close inspection.

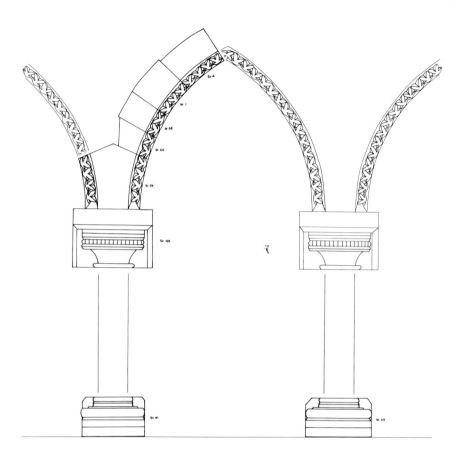

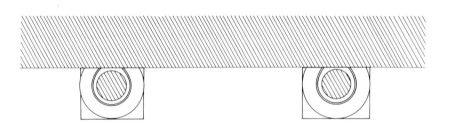

Fig 10   *The archive: reconstruction of feature to which stone recorded in Figs 8, 9, 11–14 belonged (Trust for Lincolnshire Archaeology)*

There will be three types of non-erratic line. *Continuous black lines* will represent boundaries or arrises which are still visible on the stone. *Broken black lines* will represent boundaries or arrises which are demonstrable or presumed. To some extent this will be a matter of interpretation, so these lines are always suggestions. Wherever possible they will be taken from similar examples; these parallels, and any other evidence for the suggested boundary, will be noted on the record card. *Dotted black lines* will represent incised lines on the surface of the stone where it is evident that they have been made with purpose. This line type will be used to record the positions of masons' marks, which may also be given their own separate record (Fig 11). There is no option for recording presumed incised lines on the master drawing, but missing lines in a mason's mark may be suggested in the separate register of such marks.

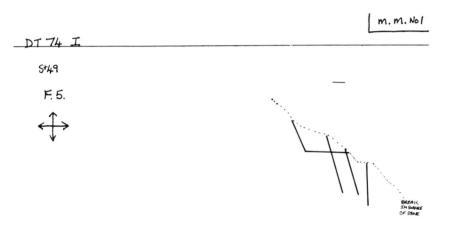

Fig 11   The archive: record card for index of masons' marks (Trust for Lincolnshire Archaeology)

34

2.2 Drawings in stipple

In a few cases there will be a need for shading or stippling. The items concerned will normally be those having some decorative carving as opposed to architectural moulding (see again the categories listed in Appendix I). In such instances drawings which make use of shading or stippling will be made *in addition* to the records drawn according to the system described in this Appendix, 2.1.

3   Photographic record (Fig 12)

Photographs should be taken of all stones for index purposes. This index, however, will *supplement* the primary drawn record in most cases.

Photographs are particularly important for fragments of sculpture, and will be used in conjunction with the drawn record to provide an adequate interpretation of such pieces. They may be used as a replacement for the drawn record only as regards the least distinguished stones (chiefly those in category 5, occasionally category 4, rarely category 3). They may also be required to record tooling in certain difficult cases (see 4, below).

Advice to photographers on taking photographs of stones appears in Appendix III.

Fig 12   The archive: index photograph (Trust for Lincolnshire Archaeology)

DT. 74 I

ST. 49

Faces 1,2,3,4,6,7

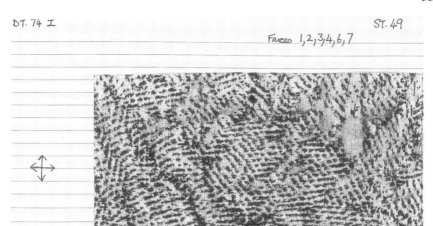

Fig 13   The archive: tooling record (rubbing) (Trust for Lincolnshire Archaeology)

Fig 14   The archive: tooling record (photograph) (Trust for Lincolnshire Archaeology)

4 Tooling (Figs 13, 14)

A rubbing, using a specialized wax and paper, will be made of each type of tooling on a stone. The sample will be of a size to ensure that a representative area is covered. It will then be mounted on a card and the following information provided: (a) site, context, and find numbers of stone; (b) the face of the stone from which the sample was taken; (c) the sample will also bear a cross (see Fig 13) to indicate the axes of the stone relative to the sample.

Tooling samples selected for publication may be either photographs of the stone or taken from the wax rubbing. It has proved possible to secure photographs of tooling direct from stones (Fig 14), but this can be time-consuming and hence is impractical for a large collection or where the stones are *in situ*. Therefore, though such photographs are highly desirable for purposes of publication, the rubbing method described above is preferred for the archive.

DRAWING A MOULDING PROFILE

A profile can be traced directly from the stone, provided that the stone is complete along the edge to be followed.

Method

Attach a sheet of paper firmly to a clipboard or drawing board laid horizontally. Place the stone on it so that the edge to be copied is in direct contact with the paper. Make sure the stone does not move while you trace. This method will work only (a) for stones which are *ex situ*; (b) for stones which are small enough to be easily handled; (c) where the profile is still complete on one edge.

For other stones, some indirect way of transferring the profile to paper needs to be adopted. One procedure is to make a measured drawing by carefully plotting various points and lines along the profile and reproducing them on squared paper. This method has its exponents (see further (3) Roberts 1977), but it is laborious.

A quicker method commonly used nowadays involves the *template former*. This consists of a row of sliding elements fixed in a central clamp (Fig 15i). The elements reproduce the contours of a surface when they are pressed up against it. Small template formers (about 150 mm wide) are generally available in good DIY shops, where they are often called 'profile gauges'. Template formers about twice this size have been specially made at the universities of East Anglia and Warwick, but are not available commercially.

Precautions

It is usually safe to use a template former on sound stone, but care should be taken if the stone is soft or friable. If the stone bears a deposit of paint it may not be advisable to use a template former at all.

Method

If you are using a small template former, several overlapping drawings will almost always be necessary to build up a complete profile. Often the former will need to be applied at two or more different planes to record all the detail faithfully (Fig 15ii).

It is not enough simply to push the template former against the stone. Holding the template former firmly with one hand so that it does not move, *all* the sliding elements should be pushed carefully against the stone with the other hand, to ensure that every detail of the profile is recorded with precision. Do not press so hard that the elements begin to spread out, as this will produce a distorted drawing (Fig 15iii). When you remove the template former from the stone surface, always check that the elements have not been forced out in this way; if they have, take that part of the profile again.

The main limitation of the small template former is in recording large continuous curved surfaces, for which several overlapping profiles will be needed. Mark points of overlap on the stone with a discreet line in chalk or pencil, and on the template former by pulling back one of the elements each time. Remember also to mark these points lightly on the drawing for guidance while making the copy (Fig 15iv). For deep concave mouldings those parts of the curved surface which the template former cannot reach should be completed by a combination of measurement and careful freehand drawing. In all cases when using a template former, check two or more dimensions on the stone after the drawing has been completed. This should be done with a rule and/or callipers, to ensure that there has been no distortion (eg in Fig 15ii: lengths A–B and C–D, and diameter E–F).

Another method
Lead wire, which can be moulded to the shape of the stone, has been successfully employed by some exponents to transfer profiles to paper. But in unskilled hands lead wire is more likely to produce distortion than the other methods. It is also rather impractical in comparison with the template former if a large number of overlapping profiles are to be recorded. However, it can be useful in supplementing the template former, especially when problems are encountered with deep hollow mouldings (see above).

Remember . . .
When tracing the outline of the profile on to paper, ensure that the pen or pencil is held at such an angle that its point follows the outline faithfully (Fig 15v). A ballpoint pen with dark ink is very suitable for such work for field drawings; it is slim in profile, and produces an indelible line with no smudging. But in damp conditions one must resort to the pencil.

After finishing the drawing, and regardless of the method that has been used, *always check it closely against the profile on the stone*. Look not only for errors and omissions, but also for lack of sharpness in small detail, especially at angles (Fig 15vi).

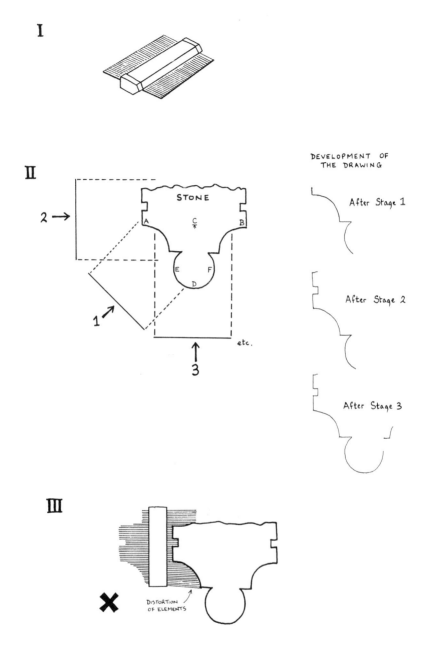

I

II

2 →

STONE

A   C   B
     *

E   F
  D

1 ↗

3 ↑

etc.

DEVELOPMENT OF
THE DRAWING

After Stage 1

After Stage 2

After Stage 3

III

✗   DISTORTION
     OF ELEMENTS

Fig 15   Steps in drawing a moulding profile using a template former (R K Morris, Warwick)

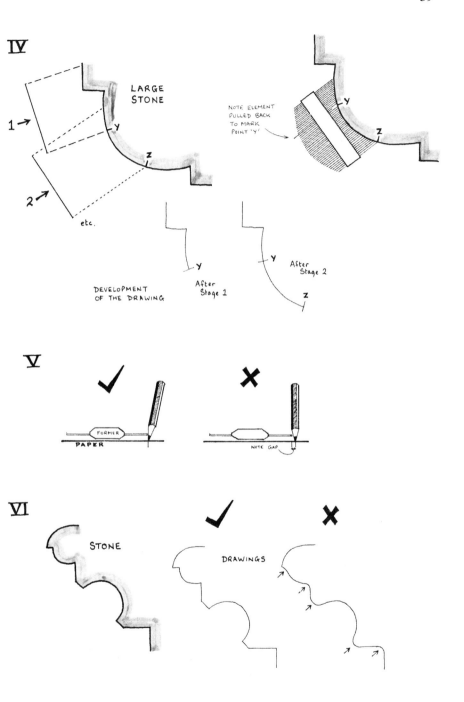

IV

LARGE
STONE

NOTE ELEMENT
PULLED BACK
TO MARK
POINT 'Y'

1→

2→

etc.

y

z

y

z

DEVELOPMENT
OF THE DRAWING

After
Stage 1

y

y

After
Stage 2

z

V

FORMER
PAPER

NOTE GAP

VI

STONE

DRAWINGS

Appendix III Taking photographs of stones

To take useful photographs of stones is not necessarily difficult, but it is unrealistic to imagine that worthwhile results can be achieved by a novice with a camera in one hand and a basic manual of photography in the other. These notes are offered as an *aide-mémoire* to photographers.

Camera type and format

The versatility offered by camera movements can be invaluable, and for certain subjects and situations nothing but a view camera will suffice. However, it is likely that it will be the more commonly available 35 mm or rollfilm SLR which is to hand, and the notes which follow are written with this in mind.

Negative area suggests that a rollfilm SLR would be preferable to a 35 mm SLR for this work – but note that Kodachrome is not yet available as rollfilm (see 'Film type') and that 'shift' lenses (see below) for rollfilm cameras are expensive.

Include identification of the subject in the photograph.   Today's gadgetry may have some applications. 'Data backs' that print information on the negative may offer a useful facility whereby a reference code and date may be included in the negative area. This can be useful for the record, but a simpler alternative – the code and date written on a card or label and placed next to the subject – achieves the same aim and also can facilitate trimming, which will remove the card from the photograph if this is desired for publication.

Use a lens of the longest focal length you can.   Choosing a lens of longer focal length than 'standard' brings the usual advantages of reducing perspective effects and facilitating effective differential focusing. Sometimes a 'shift' or 'perspective control' lens may be useful (although these are wide-angle lenses) if the camera cannot be placed at normal to the face to be photographed. A subject slightly 'lengthened' by lens movement is generally preferable to one which shows perspective effects.

Film type

That photographs of worked stone should be regarded as archival material has a bearing on the choice of film. Quite simply, photographs taken on some films available today will fade away too soon. Furthermore, prints made on present-day papers have a built-in tendency to disappear in time. If one must think in terms of priorities, permanence is more important than quality.

Aim for permanence.   For archival use, the standard type of black-and-white film is still the best. Medium-speed panchromatic films – eg Kodak Plus-X, Ilford HP5, etc – are the best choice for the 35 mm user. The photographer with a rollfilm camera may, with the larger negative, choose to reduce contrast with faster film without noticeably affecting quality. The recently introduced Ilford XP1 is technologically akin to colour film and its longevity has yet to be established.

40

Be wary of colour film. Only Kodak's Kodachrome colour positive film has proved itself suitable for long-term storage. At present (October 1984) this is available only in 35 mm size, but even with this small negative its fine grain and subtle colours produce superb results. Stick to Kodachrome 25, unless the extra stop or so of Kodachrome 64 is absolutely vital. Fuji's colour positive and HR negative films, with their tendency to violent colour, bring a sparkle to drab subjects and certainly can show stone to advantage – but the suitability of these new films for archival use is unknown.

For better negatives, rate your black-and-white films a little slower than the manufacturers suggest on the packets – Kodak Plus-X and Ilford FP4 at ISO 80–100; Kodak Tri-X and Ilford HP5 at ISO 200–320. In addition make an appropriate allowance for tungsten lighting, if used. Don't be tempted to use 'acutance' developers – stick to D-76 or ID-11.

Lighting

Clear visibility of a stone fragment does not mean that special measures to light the stone for photography should be neglected. Poor photographs are so often the result when the photographer 'makes do' with daylight alone.

If the subject is in the open air and cannot be moved to a position where natural light can show it to advantage, observe how the sun falls upon the subject throughout the day, choose the best time for the photograph and consider using white card as a reflector for fill-in light.

Use only one main light source. More than this will cause multiple shadows. To produce an easily understood likeness, the convention is for the main light to strike the subject from above the viewer's left shoulder. Do not forget fill-in light. If using flash, add this from the camera position, from immediately above the taking lens.

Flash-unit fixed to camera? If the only light source available is a small flash unit that cannot be operated away from the camera (eg 'hot shoe' flash or as with 'compact' 35 mm cameras), fit a medium wide-angle lens and move as close to the subject as possible. This will increase the effective offset between lens and light source, thus reducing the flattening of surface detail caused by direct lighting. In these circumstances colour film might be found helpful; whereas black-and-white prints give tonal differentiation, colour can show changes of hue, saturation and luminosity. Colour negative film will stand over-exposure better than colour positive and so might be a safer choice if this approach is used.

Backgrounds

Do not take scissors to your prints. Despite the photographer's best efforts, it is likely that distracting backgrounds will intrude. If differential focusing cannot isolate the subject and the use of background paper or cloth is impractical, do not be tempted to remove the unwanted background by cutting around the subject with scissors. No matter how carefully this may be done, the outline of the subject will be falsified.

Photographs of tooling call for a strong 'cutting' light, usually without fill-in. Position the light source to bring out the tool-marks clearly, ignoring the 'light from over the left shoulder' rule. Cameras with 'off-the-film' flash control will determine the correct exposure automatically (Olympus OM-2/2N, OM-3, OM-4, Nikon F3, Pentax LX and 645 are some current models which offer this facility). If you cannot visualize the effect, use a torch to determine the best position for the flash head. Flash lighting is not essential, of course, but its undiffused source is an advantage, and it can be quicker.

Tripods and camera stands

A really solid base for the camera is essential. It allows a wide choice of lens apertures for accurate depth-of-field control and best lens performance, the use of slower films, precise composition, and ease in the placing of photographic scales.

A flimsy tripod can be worse than none at all. Beware the combination of a flimsy tripod and rollfilm SLR with focal plane shutter. Even when this kind of camera offers a mirror-lift facility, a lightweight tripod is a recipe for camera shake. If a really heavy-duty professional tripod is not to hand, hire one.

Scales

Archaeologists like to include photographic scales in their photographs, which is a useful habit. Scales are easily made, small ones from wooden dowelling and larger ones from broom handles. Most practical of all, however, are scales which are square in section; they can be angled so that the surface does not catch the light, and tend to stay put. Cut scales to lengths which are standard multiples of the divisions shown on the scale: eg 12 in, not 9 in. Paint scales with alternating black and white bands to show the units (in, cm or whatever is required). The finish should be matte.

The scale should suit the subject. Generally, there is no need for the scale to be larger than the subject – indeed it looks much better if the reverse is the case. Keep a record of the units shown on the scale if there is no indication in the photograph.

Imperial or metric? It matters little. The metre, if not yet fully accepted in the British Isles, is now universally understood, and used in scientific circles. The foot is historically more meaningful but is likely to be decreasingly familiar to future generations.

Placing the scale in the photograph. Scales rarely enhance the pictorial qualities of the photograph and should be placed where they can be removed from the final print if this is necessary for publication. A more appropriate scale can be substituted by the printer if desired.

Remember that a photographic scale is only of use for direct measurement when it is placed both in the same plane as the subject and at the same distance from the camera.

Appendix IV   Records and the computer

1   Written records: storage, etc

Most archaeologists are familiar with the transfer of written records onto the computer, and many commercially available computer systems have some sort of software capable of handling this requirement with varying degrees of success. For instance, a package such as *dBase* on a microcomputer could manage small sets of data fairly successfully, but large collections pose more problems, particularly organizational ones. In considering which computer system might be most appropriate to your needs, many mundane questions need to be raised, such as efficiency of data storage, speed of retrieval, size of overall record, cost. These questions are universal to all forms of computerization, and are often not fully appreciated, even though they underlie most discussions by archaeologists of 'computerizing the record' (see (7) Richards & Ryan 1985, for an up-to-date appraisal).

2   Visual records: storage, etc

Advances in computer graphics mean that it is now viable to consider transferring the drawings directly onto the computer as 'shape data'. There are currently a few inexpensive add-on units for microcomputers which could be adapted for this task, and it seems likely that many more will become available. They take the form of either a 'digitizing tablet' or a pantograph. The former usually involves a flat board of up to half a metre in size, connected to some sort of electronic wand, pen or 'puck' which traces round a drawing taped down onto it. For this type of instrument the shape has to be transferred to paper first, since in order to work the pen must be within the area of the board and not more than a few millimetres above it. The advantage is that considerable precision can be achieved, usually in the order of tenths of millimetres, depending on cost. The cheaper, and possibly more appropriate machine is the pantograph type, which is now becoming available for many consumer microcomputers. It is similar in appearance to a child's copying pantograph, but incorporates position-sensing potentiometers at the pivot points. While not as accurate as the former type, (about 2 mm over an A4 sheet), the board does not form part of the electronics, and so the machine can be adapted to trace around shapes directly. It is well within the current 'state of the art' to produce a pantograph system capable of tracing in three dimensions; the technical skill required is certainly not beyond the resources, say, of a university department or even a dedicated amateur computer enthusiast. Indeed a large-scale system has been postulated for on-site archaeological recording (see (7), Walker 1985).

Modern computer systems are capable not only of storing shape data, but also of classifying, displaying and printing them, though more research and development are necessary for all these functions. It is particularly in the field of pottery that related techniques have been employed for a number of years (see (7) Angell & Main 1982; Main 1978; 1979).

3 Visual records: a database for research

The functions described above are likely to be of most use to the majority of archaeologists and curators. However, for further research in the visual records, a computerized database that can be interrogated is extremely useful. At present the graphics systems described above do not incorporate a programme capable of carrying out sophisticated analyses and comparisons of the constituent elements in each drawing. However, current research in this area at such institutions as North Staffordshire Polytechnic and Newcastle Polytechnic means that it should be only a matter of time before such a package is available (see (7) Spicer forthcoming).

In the meantime, however, the most feasible way to compile such a database is to translate the visual records into a machine-readable code, external to the machine, and then to input this description. This is time-consuming but it allows one to make use of existing, proven software. Such work has been carried out successfully at the University of Warwick for section drawings of moulding profiles, using an adapted version of the Oxford Concordance Program. Warwick has a research archive of drawings of mouldings, based mainly on standing buildings, but also including some examples from excavated sites. The scope of the archive is mainly English, ecclesiastical, c 1250–1400, but it is planned eventually to include all major buildings in England and Wales from the mid 12th century to the early 17th century, and select examples from western Europe as well.

The Warwick Archive will produce, for example, a concordance of all the types of moulding found in one building, or a list of all the instances known to it in England and Wales of one or more moulding types. Searches can be limited by region and/or date, to the nearest quarter century, if required. Thus, useful parallels for dating, attribution and usage can often be discovered for excavated stones. The archive is available to interested parties for consultation, and acts as an international focus for matters relating to the recording and analysis of medieval mouldings (see 'Contact addresses').

4 Priorities

A computer system functioning properly, with a competent operator, can save considerable time, labour and storage space, particularly for written records. However, it will not solve the basic problems which this book has set out to address; such solutions can be provided only by skilled personnel working directly with the stones. Therefore, there is usually no advantage to be gained at present by rushing into computerization for the sake of being up-to-date, especially as computer systems continue to improve in specification and decrease in relative cost at bewildering speed. Furthermore, it should be borne in mind that *initially* the operating of a computer system to compile records is almost always more time-consuming than traditional methods. If resources are limited and there is a backlog of stones to be catalogued, the priority should normally be to devote such time and money as are available to the continuation of recording by traditional methods.

Contact addresses

Computing

Dr R K Morris, Warwick Archive of Mouldings, Department of History of Art, University of Warwick, Coventry, CV4 7AL, tel 0203 24011

Department of Computing, North Staffordshire Polytechnic, Blackheath Lane, Stafford, ST18 0AD, tel 0785 53511 ex 59

Conservation

Conservation Officer, Council for the Care of Churches, 83 London Wall, London, EC2M 5NA, tel 01 638 0971

Seamus Hanna, Senior Conservator Stone Section, Conservation Division, British Museum, London, WC1B 3DG, tel 01 636 1555 ex 346

John Larson, Victoria & Albert Museum, Cromwell Road, London, SW7 2RL, tel 01 589 6371

Acknowledgements

The Working Party wishes to record its gratitude to the following, who offered constructive criticism and advice: Archaeology Section, United Kingdom Institute of Conservation; Alan Carter (Norwich Survey); Seamus Hanna and N J Lee (Conservation Division, British Museum); Helen Humphries; Robert Janaway; John Larson (Victoria & Albert Museum); Nicholas Moore (HBMC); Sonia O'Connor; Dick Spicer (Department of Computing, N Staffordshire Polytechnic); Jim Spriggs (York Archaeological Trust); Susan White; Francis Woodman (Norwich Survey). Responsibility for the views expressed within the manual rests with the Working Party.

Bibliography

1 General

Bond, F, 1905 *Gothic architecture in England*
Clifton-Taylor, A, 1972 *The pattern of English building*
Harvey, J H, 1969 Conservation of old buildings: a select bibliography, *Trans Ancient Monuments Soc*, **16**
Rodwell, W, 1981 *The archaeology of the English church*
Salzman, L F, 1967 *Building in England down to 1540*, 2 edn

2 Stones and stonemasonry

Blagg, T C F, 1976 Tools and techniques of the Roman stone mason in Britain, *Britannia*, **7**, 152–72
Clifton-Taylor, A, & Ireson, A, 1983 *English stone building*
Davey, N, 1961 *A history of building materials*
———, 1976 *Building stones of England and Wales*
Davis, R H C, 1954 A catalogue of masons' marks as an aid to architectural history, *J Brit Archaeol Assoc*, 3 ser, **17**, 43–76
Harvey, J H, 1972 *The mediaeval architect*
———, 1975 *Mediaeval craftsmen*
Hill, P R, 1981 Stonework and the archaeologist, *Archaeol Aeliana*, 5 ser, **9**, 1–22
Hudson, K, 1971 *The fashionable stone*
Jope, E M, 1964 The Saxon building stone industry in southern and midland England, *Medieval Archaeol*, **8**, 91–118
Knoop, D, & Jones, J P, 1932 Masons and apprenticeship in medieval England, *Econ Hist Rev*, **3**, 346 ff
———, 1933 *The medieval mason*
———, 1938 The English medieval quarry, *Econ Hist Rev*, **9**, 17–37
Stocker, D, forthcoming *The college of the Vicars Choral, York: the architectural evidence* (see Appendix 1, which covers tooling studies generally)
Warland, E G, 1928 *Modern practical masonry*
Warnes, A, 1926 *Building stones: their properties, decay and preservation*
Watson, J, 1911 *British and foreign building stones*

3 Moulding analysis

Bond, F, 1905 *Gothic architecture in England*, esp 658–707 (one of the most useful selections, drawn from a variety of earlier books; generally accurate)
Borg, A, 1967 The development of chevron ornament, *J Brit Archaeol Soc*, 3 ser, **30**, 122–40
Forrester, H, 1972 *Medieval Gothic mouldings* (mouldings discussed by type, but antiquarian in approach; drawings of examples prone to error and simplification)
Harvey, J H, 1978 *The Perpendicular style* (useful collection of drawings of national examples from the late Gothic period, in an Appendix and interspersed with the text)
Johnson, P M, 1924 Romanesque ornament in England, *J Brit Archaeol Assoc*, 2 ser, **30**, 91–104
Morris, R K, 1978, 1979 The development of later Gothic mouldings in England *c* 1250–1400, *Architect Hist*, **21**, 18–57; **22**, 1–48 (typological development of mouldings from the Decorated and early Perpendicular periods in their northern European context)
Paley, F A, 1865 *A manual of Gothic mouldings*, 3 edn (the most common of the antiquarian handbooks; still important, but limited in its interpretational value)
Rigold, S, 1977 Romanesque bases in and south-east of the limestone belt, in *Ancient monuments and their interpretation* (eds M Apted *et al*), 99–137 (valuable typological catalogue for southern England)

Roberts, E, 1977 Moulding analysis and architectural research: the late middle ages, *Architect Hist*, **20**, 5–13. (a short history of the use of mouldings to identify the styles of individual masons)

Sharpe, E, 1848 *Architectural parallels*

——, 1871–4 *The mouldings of the six periods of British architecture from the Conquest to the Reformation* (the finest of the 19th century publications on mouldings, but both rare books)

4 Architectural sculpture

Cave, C J P, 1948 *Roof bosses in medieval churches*

Cocke, T, *et al* 1984, *Recording a church: an illustrated glossary*, CBA

Gardner, S, 1927 *English Gothic foliage sculpture*

Prior, E S & Gardner, A, 1912 *An account of medieval figure sculpture in England*

Stone, L, 1972 *Sculpture in Britain: the middle ages*, 2 edn

Taylor, H M & J, 1966 Architectural sculpture in pre-Norman England, *J Brit Archaeol Assoc*, 3 ser, **29**, 3–51

Zarnecki, G, 1951 *English Romanesque Sculpture 1066–1140*

——, 1953 *English Romanesque Sculpture 1140–1210*

—— & Henry, F, 1957 Romanesque arches decorated with human and animal heads, *J Brit Archaeol Soc*, 3 ser, **20**, 1–34

——, 1966 1066 and architectural sculpture, *Proc Brit Acad*, **52**, 87–104

5 Conservation

CCC, 1985 *Loose stones: sculptural and architectural fragments in churches*, Council for the Care of Churches

Dowman, E A, 1970 *Conservation in field archaeology*

Leigh, D, 1978 *First aid for finds*, Rescue, 2 edn (3 edn forthcoming)

Longworth, I H, (ed), 1982 *Selection and retention of environmental and artefactual material from excavations. A report by a working party of the British Museum*

Massan, G, 1971 *Humidity in monuments*, ICCROM

Stambolov, T, & van Asperen de Boer, J R J, 1972 *The deterioration and conservation of porous building materials in monuments*, ICCROM

Torraca, G, 1981 *Porous building materials: material science for architectural conservation*, ICCROM

UKIC, 1983 *Packaging and storage of freshly excavated artefacts from archaeological sites*, Conservation guidelines 2

UKIC, 1984 *Environmental standards for the permanent storage of excavated material from archaeological sites*, Conservation guidelines 3

6 Health and safety

British Safety Council, 1970 *Safe slinging, safe lifting: an illustrated guide*

CBA, 1972 *Responsibility and safeguards in archaeological excavation*

Health and safety at work Act 1974 (see also scaffolding regulations)

HMSO, 1975 *Lifting and carrying*, Health and safety at work 1

7 Computer applications

Angell, I O, & Main, P L, 1982 A construction of 3-dimensional views from the silhouette data of pottery, *Proc Ann Conference on Computer Applications in Archaeol* (Bradford), 117–28

——, 1978 The storage, retrieval and classification of artifact shapes, *Proc Ann Conference on Computer Applications in Archaeol* (Birmingham), 39–49

Main, P L, 1979 Desirable attributes for a data-bank of archaeological shapes, *ibid*, 5–13

Richards, J D, & Ryan, N, 1985 *Data processing in archaeology*

Spicer, R D, forthcoming Stereoscopic presentation of archaeological data, *Sci & Archaeol*

Walker, R, 1985 Computerized planning in archaeology, *Unpubl paper to Computer Applications in Archaeology Conference 1985*